JEFF WALL – TRANSPARENCIES

Jeff Wall's pictures are not photographs or conventional images on a screen: they are Cibachrome transparencies lit from within by fluorescent light. Their appearance, which is reminiscent of illuminated advertising displays, exercizes a singular fascination on the viewer: they have an immediate visual impact, and the images which they present have a disturbing, unsettling effect. The seemingly familiar world which Jeff Wall's figures inhabit is a deliberately constructed "reality", the product of a subtle and elaborately detailed *mise-en-scène.*

Born in 1946, Jeff Wall is associate professor in Visual Art at the Centre for the Arts, Simon Fraser University, Vancouver BC, Canada. In the interview with Els Barents published here he discusses the relationship of his work to specific art-historical sources, to the intellectual, political and aesthetic traditions of the avant-garde, and to the pictorialism of contemporary mass culture.

This book is the first substantial illustrated volume devoted to Jeff Wall's work.

Movie Audience 1979 (L), Stereo 1980. Installation Kunsthalle Basel 1984

Jeff Wall
TRANSPARENCIES

With an interview by Els Barents

RIZZOLI NEW YORK

Design: Rodney Graham.
A Schirmer/Mosel Production.

PLATES

Details are reproduced to size of original enlargements.

The Destroyed Room 1978

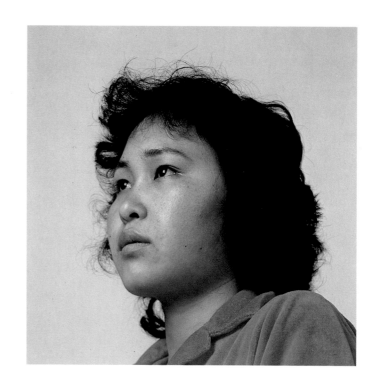

Young Workers 1978—83

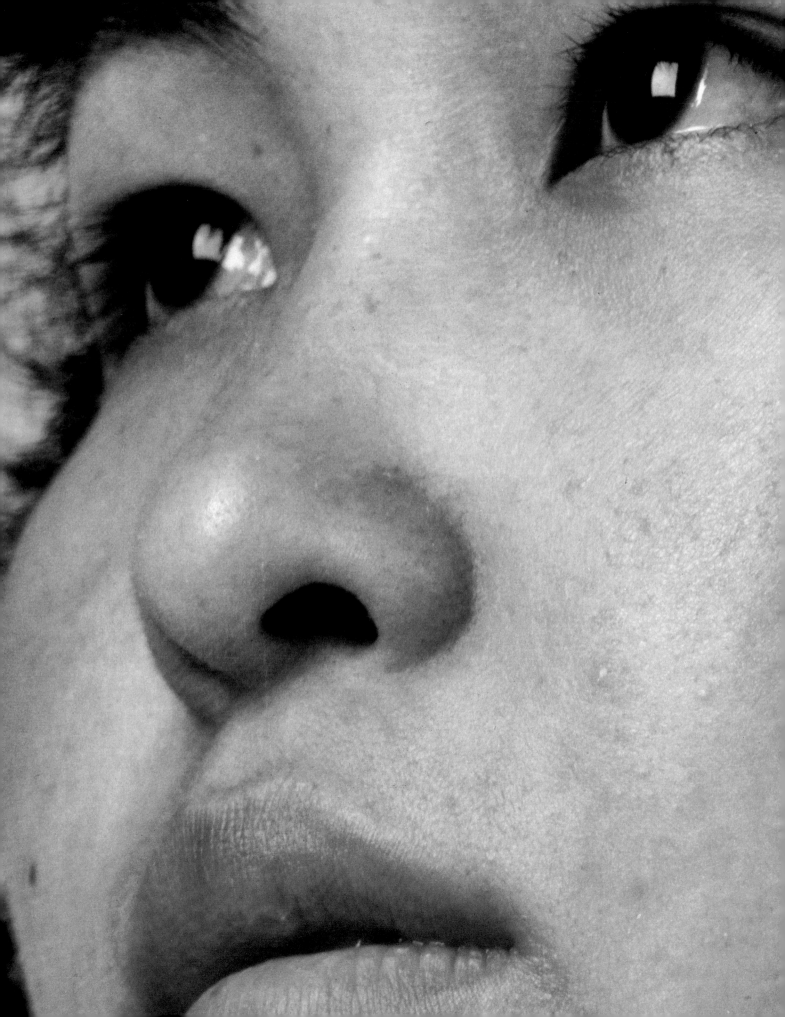

Picture for Women 1979

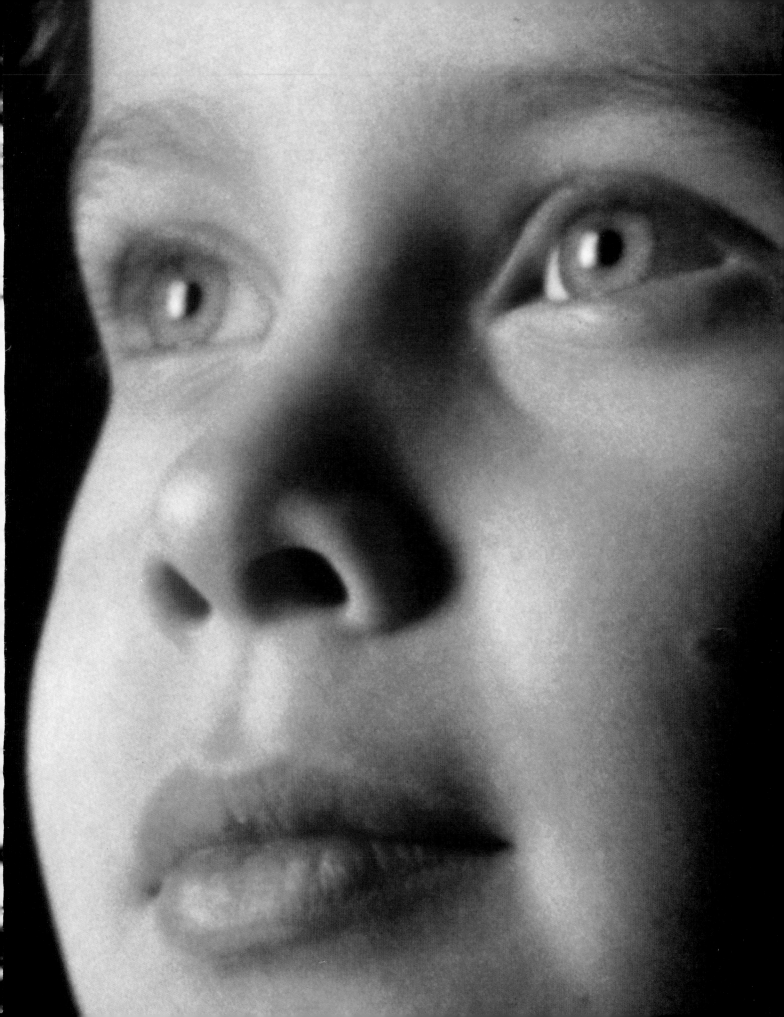

Movie Audience 1979

Double Self-Portrait 1979

STEREO

Stereo 1980

Steves Farm, Steveston 1980

The Jewish Cemetery 1980

The Bridge 1980

Woman and her Doctor 1980–81

Backpack 1981–82

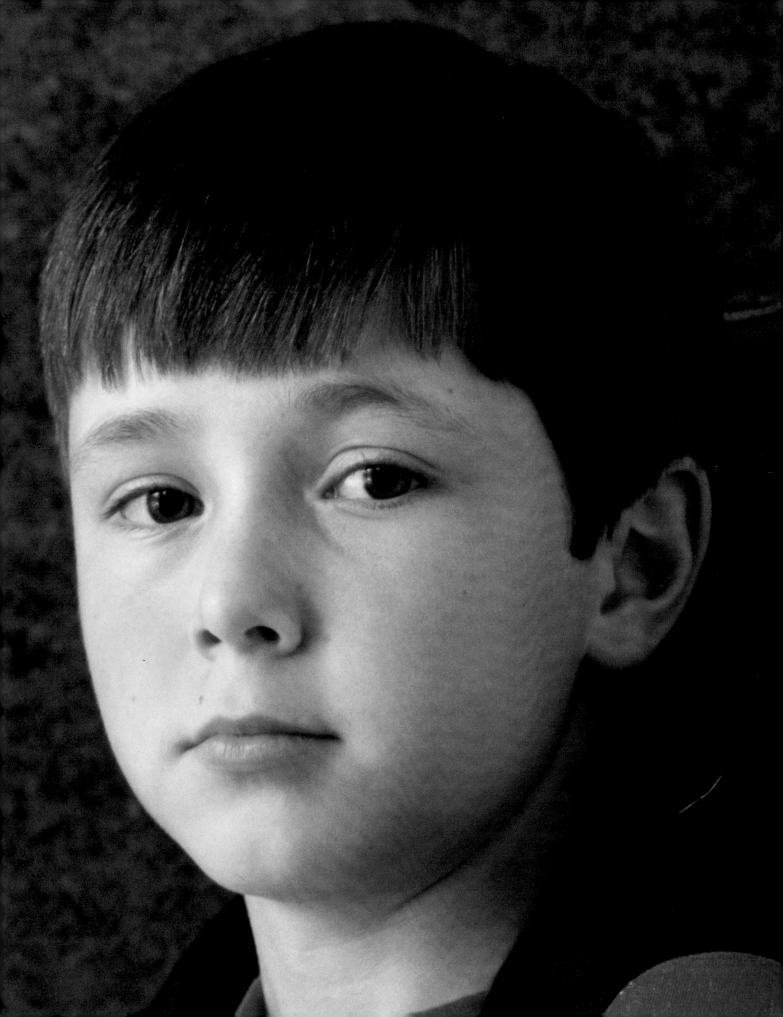

Mimic 1982

No 1983

Doorpusher 1984

Bad Goods 1984

Milk 1984

Diatribe 1985

Abundance 1985

The Smoker 1986

The Thinker 1986.

Backpack 1981–82 (L), Double Self-Portrait 1979. Installation The Renaissance Society, Chicago 1983

Double Self-Portrait 1979 (L), Mimic 1982. Installation The Renaissance Society, Chicago 1983

No 1983 (L), Bad Goods 1984. Installation Biennale de Paris 1985

The Smoker 1986. Installation Galerie Johnen & Schöttle, Köln 1986

TYPOLOGY, LUMINESCENCE, FREEDOM
Selections from a conversation with Jeff Wall

Jeff Wall is an artist, art historian and teacher. He lives and works in Vancouver, Canada, where he was born. His work has become known in Europe since 1981 through his inclusion in such exhibitions as *Westkunst, Documenta 7, Nouvelle Biennale de Paris,* and in several solo shows. The interview published here was carried out on the nights preceding the opening of his exhibition at the Stedelijk Museum in Amsterdam in September 1985.

In his work, Wall has created a complex relationship between historical knowledge and the current state of society, between the effects of high art and those of advanced technology. He wants to confront high art with the sensuality and the pictorialism of mass culture and mass culture with the intellectual, political and aesthetic traditions of the avant-garde.

His pictures are characterized by great attention to sub-ject, detail, composition and technique. The dramatization of his subjects is rooted in a process of meticulous construction of appearances through a method akin to both cinematography and traditional oil painting. In this, he is attempting to establish strictly contemporary terms for a recovery of the qualities and functions of the older pictorial art which he considers a still-living part of culture.

In the interview, Wall discusses his intention to interrelate the diverse aspects of his production and his intellectual reflection on it. He considers theory to be essential to the development of his work. He believes that the process of illumination of practice by cultural theory distinguishes critical aesthetics from those attitudes which begin from the idea of the "end of the avant-garde" and end in reconciliation with official forms of culture and thought.

Els Barents

TYPOLOGY

Els Barents: Since 1978 you've produced 20 works. In some early pieces, particularly *The Destroyed Room* (1978) and *Picture for Women* (1979), you related your pictures to specific art-historical sources. But more recently your attitude toward this procedure seems to have changed. The emphatic connection to specific historical works of modernist art seems to have mutated, if not disappeared.

Jeff Wall: In my earlier pictures I was trying to be a little more dogmatic, trying to establish my position, my theoretical relations with conceptual art and through that with what I think of as an avant-garde "counter-tradition". This was in 1978, at the beginning of the new painting. It was a new subjectivistic period, and I was in certain ways trying to hold out against it, trying to con-tinue an idea of historically and theoretically informed production, an idea which was, at that time at least, being identified with a failed cultural politics – that of the 60s and 70s – a defunct, nostalgic avant-gardism. When I first started making these photographs I thought it was important to make a definite reference to other works. For example, when I made *The Destroyed Room,* I worked in reference to the design of commercial window displays of clothing and furniture. I think of these as *tableaux morts* as opposed to *tableaux vivants.* At the time, they had become very violent, mainly because of an influence from the punk phenomenon which was quickly filtering into the whole cultural economy. At the same time, the picture's subject matter had something to do with aggression, violence and revenge in domestic

Eugène Delacroix: ›La mort de Sardanapal‹, 1827. 395 × 495 cm. Musée du Louvre, Paris.

life. I was very interested in Delacroix's *Death of Sardanapalus,* partly because I was lecturing on Romanticism. I think the *Sardanapalus* is a very important picture, historically and psychologically, because it shows the eroticized ideal of military glory which characterized the Napoleonic period being turned inward, back toward domestic life at the end of that epoch, at the beginning of modern, bourgeois, neurotic private life. This painting interested me as a kind of crystal. My subject was made with this crystal, by passing my ideas and feelings through the historical prism of another work. I felt that this made the subject richer, more suggestive, more

Edouard Manet: ›Un bar aux Folies-Bergères‹, 1881–82. 96 × 130 cm. Courtauld Institute Galleries (Home House Trustees), London.

aggressive. It was important to filter *The Destroyed Room* through this other picture because I think I was trying to establish a space for myself by suggesting which historical directions and problems were important to me. I know that in some ways this is a very artifical way of going about things, very manneristic even, but it was a way to begin, and I had to begin.

Els Barents: But people can respond to *The Destroyed Room* without having to be familiar with Delacroix's picture. *Picture for Women* is different; it seems to be so strongly related to Manet's painting *The Bar in the Folies-Bergères* that one can't really appreciate it without engaging in some kind of art-historical or cultural study.

Jeff Wall: Picture for Women is a "remake" of Manet's picture. *The Bar* had really impressed me; I'd seen it repeatedly in the Courtauld Galleries in London when I was a student. I wanted to comment on it, to analyze it in a new picture, to try to draw out of it its inner structure, that famous positioning of figures, male and female, in an everyday working situation which was also a situation of spectacularity, that regime of distraction and entertainment which Manet dealt with. I made my picture as a theoretical diagram in an empty classroom. Maybe for Manet this spectacular regime was something immediate; but at the time I made *Picture for Women* these things had become openly theoretical, political issues, mainly through the influence of the women's movement in the art world. There were lessons being learned throughout the period, so maybe the classroom setting has something to do with this. I think that, at that time, it was not so unusual to be bringing together a kind of theoretical activity – study, if you like – with the enjoyment of pictures.

It was also a remake the way that movies are remade. The same script is reworked and the appearance, the style, the semiotics, of the earlier film are subjected to a commentary in the new version. This dialectic interests me. It's a judgement on which elements of the past are still alive. It's standard procedure in the theatre, where the same plays are produced over and over again, interminably. And as long as painting remains "painted drama" – which it always does, in my opinion – then these issues of the dramas of the past and their representations in the present, whether staged or painted or photographed, must be at the centre of the problematics of painting and its relations with other technologies of representation.

It's true, as you say, that my more recent pictures don't

really have this relation to a specific work. The relations seem now to be more to pictorial typologies, generic structures or laws which appear as modes of spatial organization, types of figure-ground relations and things like that.

Els Barents: Works like *No* and *Milk,* for example, are dramatic. A sense of dramatized meaning is very evident in them. A more recent work, *Diatribe,* on the other hand, seems very undramatic, even ordinary. Yet I know you value it highly. During some of our talks you claimed that it has a generic relation to classicistic art. How does this picture work with pictorial typologies?

Jeff Wall: With *Diatribe,* I wanted to make a picture of a group in the street. I've done a sort of series of these "street pictures", beginning with *Mimic* in 1982. It was not clear to me beforehand just what I wanted the picture to look like. I don't like to repeat myself formally; I prefer each subject to also propose a certain kind of picture. Pictorial typology and the range of subjects is linked, too, I think.

When I'm making a picture, I spend a lot of time in my car driving around the city, "location scouting". I'm usually looking for a certain combination of elements, a kind of street, certain architectural typologies and so on. Naturally, I always search with something specific in mind. But this idea, which is usually the early concept of the picture, is quite abstract and indistinct. So searching tends to become wandering, a kind of *flânerie* which is conducive to musing. In this process the concept becomes more sensuous, gets related to a real mood, and finally to an actual place. This place is always more complex spatially or pictorially than I had first imagined it, always far more interesting and rich in suggestion. For example, in *Milk,* I had thought of the figure against a blank wall. But the actual site is far more differentiated, and the gap between the buildings has for me an effect similar to the unexpected openings in the perspective of mannerist paintings. The same kinds of things occur in working out the people, the costumes, the objects. Sometimes the location is the first thing established, sometimes it's a person, even an object, like the headphones in *Stereo.* The picture gets made as these elements are concretized. It's a construction made out of a complex of real things, all of which are at the same time symbolic.

Sometimes a place has become fixed in my memory – maybe for many years – and a specific picture turns out to have been kindled by that memory. That was the case with *Doorpusher,* where the battered and burned door – this door which seems to be sinking back into the wall – was one I'd seen repeatedly for seven or eight years. It was at the back of the studio building where I teach. I'd often pass it after dark, fatigued from the classes that day, but with my mind racing the way it does after long discussions with students. When I began *Doorpusher,* I searched all over town for appropriate doors, making Polaroids of them, until I realized that this door had been in the picture all along. Something similar occurred with the basement setting of *Abundance.* It's in the same building. So anyway, for *Diatribe,* I was looking for a straight road at the edge of the city, and I couldn't find one. Then finally I saw this curved lane and thought "this is it". It's like something is in the back of your mind, you don't know it in advance, but you recognize it when you actually experience it. That's why wandering is important; the unconscious gets to play, the whole personality is involved and you get away from planning and a sort of narrow decision-making kind of behaviour. I think this is particularly important for me because my technique has to be so rational and calculated. Art isn't that rational even if it appears to be.

When I recognized this space, this lane, I recognized a whole lot of other things that I wanted in the picture which I wasn't aware of before. I realized that this road set up a spatial situation that strongly recalled the classical landscapes of Poussin. He rarely, if ever, uses sharp perspectival recession because it's too dramatic, too irrational. Poussin knew that the vanishing point of the perspective system is the irrational point which permits

Nicolas Poussin: ›Paysage avec Diogène‹, 1648 (?). 160 × 221 cm. Musée du Louvre, Paris.

you to call the whole rational structure into question, and so he usually hides it, as all classicists do. He always likes to have quite flat planes overlapping to produce a gently receding space, a sober, measured kind of poetry typical of classical composition.

The subject of *Diatribe* is talking and walking. The Socratic ideal of knowledge includes the idea of the peripatetic character of philosophy. Socrates strolled about the polis, meeting people in an everyday urban context, and having conversations with them. Diogenes did the same. Nietzsche took up the same idea, and was thinking of Socrates when he said that philosophizing should never be done sitting down. For this strolling philosophy, the experience of the city, of the marketplace and the public spaces which invite encounters, was seen to stimulate thought. In the past, of course, this thought has always been male, or has been identified with a male producer, a "philosopher". I liked the idea that it would now be these young, impoverished mothers, who aren't identified with philosophical knowledge and critique, who would be enacting this.

The picture was set off by seeing a group like this – one woman vehemently talking to the other. I began studying these young mothers, mostly living on welfare. I parked near playgrounds, clinics, supermarkets and laundries. I noticed that these women had become quite invisible on the street. People ignore them. They seem to have become emblematic of some insoluble contradictions. Working-class family life can never correspond to the bourgeois model set for it by the capitalist state. Even the recently ended period of prosperity didn't really transform the working class into a part of the bourgeoisie as many critics insisted. Wage-slavery and "the reserve army of labour", the unemployed who depend on the state, are still here in force. The norms imposed by the state bureaucracies are never attained by workers, particularly those at the bottom. The imposition leads only to further aggravation, only makes the miserable dilemma of the ideal of the family under the conditions of wage-labour more acute. Proletarian maternity is just as much a bourgeois scandal as proletarian prostitution is, but it's just the other side of the same coin. Prostitution is always directly spectacular; maternity is only spectacular if it can be eroticized, either with religious symbolism or with violence, or both together. The only impoverished mothers who are spectacularized today are those who disintegrate in violence of some kind, or else the "super-madonnas". For the rest, that is for almost all, it's the opposite, invisibility. They've become almost like pariahs, in terms of the public space anyway. Like Socrates, Diogenes was a public nuisance. I've always been amused by his aphorism, "In a rich man's house the only place to spit is in his face." Diogenes seems to have accepted the fact that philosophical knowledge and approval from above could not be reconciled in the kind of class society he lived in. He performed as one of society's "least-favoured members". Sartre said that the truth about society could be expressed only through the eyes of its least-favoured members. It seemed to me that these women were in such a position. So they have a generic, objective relation to the traditional aims of critical philosophy. Thus I could represent them, typologically, through the classicistic structuring of the picture, as engaged in such discourse.

So the women coming around the curve in the road and the space resolving itself in a classicistic way suggest to me the relationship between critical antiquity and critical modernity. The title word, "diatribe", comes from Greek and defines at least two ancient forms of critique – a "vehement denunciation", and a "rhetorical argument with an absent third party". I didn't become conscious of this inner content of the picture until I had actually discovered this particular space in my own process of moving through the city.

It is the meanings of the typology of pictures which makes these significations possible and objective. This typology is a material means, it's a material part of the process of making pictures, not just an arbitrary intellectualization. All my pictures are made like this. *Diatribe* is a more or less typical case.

Els Barents: The technological form of back-lit transparencies is a sort of "super-photography". It relates to aspects of mass spectacle as well as to bureaucratic ways of presenting information. Your metal boxes emit a light which makes the images very absorbing, and because the photography is so clear we are invited to look at the pictures very closely. But at the same time, they seem to be immaterial projections that can be seen just as well from a distance. Despite their very realistic subject-matter, the transparencies have a dreamlike presence. The intensity of color and light and the large scale of the works creates a dimension that's hard to describe. I know you place great importance on the interconnections between different technologies that create this effect, and also on the interconnections between these technologies and the art of painting, which you admire tremendously. How did you develop this set of connections for yourself?

Jeff Wall: I hadn't been to Europe for four or five years since I lived there in the early 70s. Then in 1977 I went back for a holiday with my family. Among other museums, I visited the Prado for the first time and looked at Velazquez, Goya, Titian. I remember coming back to Vancouver and thinking once again how powerful those pictures were, how much I loved them. And also, how they contained innumerable traces of their own modernity.

But I also felt that it was impossible to return to anything resembling the idea of the "painter of modern life", as Baudelaire termed it. And yet I think that in many ways for modernism that's a fundamental term, "the painter of modern life". Because there is no more appropriate occupation. It's a complete occupation because the art form, painting, is the greatest art form and the subject is the greatest subject. But, as I said, I felt very strongly at that time that it was impossible, because painting as an art form did not encounter directly enough the problem of the technological product which had so extensively usurped its place and its function in the representation of everyday life. It's interesting because of course this was just at the time when a lot of young artists were rediscovering painting. I remember being in a kind of crisis at the time, wondering what I would do. Just at that moment I saw an illuminated sign somewhere, and it struck me very strongly that here was the perfect synthetic technology for me. It was not photography, it was not cinema, it was not painting, it was not propaganda, but it has strong associations with them all. It was something extremely open. It seemed to be the technique in which this problem could be expressed, maybe the only technique because of its fundamental spectacularity. That satisfied the primary expectation of the product of technology, which is that it represents by means of the spectacle.

I think there's a basic fascination in technology which derives from the fact that there's always a hidden space – a control room, a projection booth, a source of light of some kind – from which the image comes. A painting on canvas, no matter how good it is, is to our eyes more or less flat, or at least flatter than the luminescent image of cinema, television, or the transparencies. One of the reasons for this is that the painting or the ordinary photograph is lit with the same light that falls in the room and onto the spectator him- or herself. But the luminescent image is fascinating because it's lit with another atmosphere. So two atmospheres intersect to make the image. One of them, the hidden one, is more powerful than the other. In a painting, for example, the source or the site of the image is palpably in front of you. You can actually touch the place where the image comes from, where it is. But in a luminescent picture the source of the image is hidden and the thing is a dematerialized or semi-dematerialized projection. The site from which the image originates is always elsewhere. And this "elsewhere" is experienced, maybe consciously, maybe not, in experiencing the image. Rimbaud said "Existence is elsewhere", and Malevich once wrote, "Only that which cannot be touched can be sacred". To me, this experience of two places, two worlds, in one moment is a central form of the experience of modernity. It's an experience of dissociation, of alienation. In it, space – the space inside and outside of the picture – is experienced as it really exists in capitalism: there is always a point of control, of projection, which is inaccessible. It is a classical site of power. I see it as an analogue of capitalist social relations, which are relations of dissociation. We are permitted to play the game of transformation of nature, the great festival of metamorphosis, only by going through capital, by being subjected to the laws of capital. For example, you can't turn seeds into plants without going through, or into, capital. Ask any farmer. Something becomes inaccessible to us as we work on it. Thus we are both in the game and separated from it at the same time. The technological product, as we currently experience it from within capitalism, recapitulates this situation in its experiential structure, which gives us something very intensely and at the same time makes it remote.

Furthermore, the fascination of this technology for me is that it seems that it alone permits me to make pictures in the traditional way. Because that's basically what I do, although I hope it is done with an effect that is opposite to that of technically traditional pictures. The opportunity is both to recuperate the past – the great art of the museums – and at the same time to participate with a critical effect in the most up-to-date spectacularity. This gives my work its particular relation to painting. I like to think that my pictures are a specific opposite to painting.

Els Barents: Before you began to make these transparencies you were for some years very interested in making films. You had no success in that, but it has obviously had a strong influence on how you approach your still pictures.

Jeff Wall: I think that the process of film-making is in important ways analogous to the methods of painting, at least to those aspects of painting which interest me the most. I'm referring to the regulated aspects of an art form, those which have the function of the public or social construction of meaning, as opposed to the more immediately expressive factors. Regulation implies a regulating force, an institution. Institutionalization always implies repetition. Repetition is maybe the foundation of institutionalization. Regulation, repetition, formalization, abstraction. These are the basic modernist, bureaucratic approaches to things.

The starting point of a normal, commercial film is usually quite abstract – a business deal, some market projections. The process of concretization develops through a pretty formalized division of labour, and so conventionalized methods operate at every stage: lighting codes, set design, acting technique, casting services, etc. This bureaucratic, and hence theoretically informed cooperation resembles the production processes of the old academic fine arts. The old academies are the prototypes of corporate cultural production and corporate, regulated products, just as much as the idea of the factory is. So in such situations the image is the outcome of a complex division of labour. The idea of individual artistic imagination, or creativity, isn't dispensed with, as structuralists and other positivists claim, but is plunged realistically into the actual world of social relationships, particularly the antagonistic and objectivistic relationships involved in the production of value in capitalism. Both the corporatized painter of the past and the filmmaker now are obliged to transform the incessant abstractionism of the modern production process into a work of art. That's an old struggle, the struggle with the historically evolved social forms of production, which tend toward conventionalization, simplification, and formulaic repetition. The struggle is to realize something unique, profound, sensuous and true through the actual movement of socialized abstractions, which are directed away from these qualities, toward maybe a kind of emptiness. But society contains this emptiness and its opposite, and both appear in the work of art. To me, cinematography consists in this extreme paradox, this photographing of abstractions in the dream of producing the opposite out of them. This dialectic appeals to me because it isn't limited by any ideas of the spontaneous production of the effect of life in the image. The spontaneous is the most beautiful thing that can appear in a picture, but nothing in art appears less spontaneously than that.

So I think that cinematography is aesthetically more developed than the more spontaneous photographic aesthetic, the one identified with Cartier-Bresson for example. The reliance on immediate spontaneity thins out the image, reduces the level at which the permanent dialectic between essence and appearance operates in it. Although the picture which is made is often very meaningful and beautiful, I'm not convinced that the beauty isn't in a way limited by its dependence on the immediate surface of things. That kind of photography becomes a version of *art informel;* despite its formal richness, it is condemned always to gaze at the world in wonder and irony rather than engage in construction.

I also think that, artistically, photography established itself on the basis of cinema, and not the other way around. This has to do with the interconnections between cinema, painting, theatre, and photography. Ian Wallace and I have spent a lot of time talking about the fact that once cinema emerged, the narrativity that had previously been the property of painting was expelled from it. Until this time, painting was quite explicitly painted drama, and so it was always in a multivalent relationship with theatrical ideas. Our pictorial experience of drama was created by painting, drawing, etching, and so on. But the cinema, unlike the forms of performance it canned and played back, is a performance picture. Cinema synthesized the functions of painting and of theatre simultaneously on the technical basis of photographic reproduction. So in that synthesis the mechanics of photography were invested with tremendous meaning, a meaning they will now always have.

FREEDOM

Els Barents: Your view of society is not really a pleasant or happy one, it seems. Your figures are always under some kind of pressure or restraint, no one seems to be doing what they want to be doing in life. Your world appears to be ruled by an iron hand. There are a lot of laws in it. But you talk about how society contains opposites always. How do you think this "opposite" manifests itself in your pictures?

Jeff Wall: I'm aware that my pictures have a feeling of unfreedom about them. Their subject matter is unfreedom, too. The form and the technique tend to have a hyper-organized, rigid character, everything is strictly positioned. I want to express the existing unfreedom in the most realistic way. Take for example *Bad Goods.* This picture is constructed as a kind of triangle, one point of which is outside the image. The heap of rotting lettuces is the apex, and the two other corners are made up of the British Columbia Indian in the picture, and the spectator in front of it. Both the spectator and the Indian are looking at the lettuces and at each other. But their social relation to that lettuce may be different. I say "maybe" because the audience for pictures is changing as the economy worsens. Some spectators are getting a lot richer, some maybe poorer. The Indian may need some of the lettuce to eat. If so, he'll have to scrounge through it and find what is not rotten. His view of the lettuce is partially determined by his class position, by his poverty, which is quite typical of, in this case, the native Indian people in British Columbia, where I live. Many of them exist in the city apparently as victims of modernization, of development, of "progress", of capitalism. They are often depicted as just that, victims of capitalism, and not much more. I fear and dislike these sorts of representation. But this Indian, in my view, will never move toward the lettuce as long as the spectator is also there, as long as the triangle exists. This triangle separates two people from each other and in doing that it is a kind of diagram of the consequences of the economy. In the economy natural products separate people from each other because they are also always forms capital takes. Lettuce,

like any commodity, is just capital in a kind of natural disguise. Ideally, humans are united over food. But I suppose that presumes there's food for everyone. The Indian will not move toward the lettuce, he will not be seen as just a victim, as a "beggar" or whatever category you want to set up. He will not perform. That is his performance. His unfreedom is more important to him than food. He is not just a victim, he is also a fighter. In *Bad Goods* the whole structure of the picture is based on this figure's necessary unfreedom, and his expression of it. The only concept of freedom in it is, I guess, Hegel's: freedom is the rational recognition of necessity.

In my pictures feeling, too, is heavily constrained. I think that every figure I have made is filled with suppressed emotion, which isn't allowed to be seen directly. In *Milk,* for example, the man's body is tense and rigid with inexpressivity. It's the object which is exploding. In my pictures there is a lot of non-gesturing, or very small, compulsive gesturing, what I call "micro-gesture". The men's gestures in *No* or *Mimic* are micro-gestures. These are gestures which seem automatic, mechanical, or compulsive. They well up from somewhere deeply social, somewhere I don't primarily identify with the individual's unconscious as such. The abusive white lumpenproletarian in *Mimic,* for example, is making a gesture, pulling up his eyelid in a mimesis of the Oriental eye. In my dramatization of it for myself, I thought of it happening so quickly that nobody in the picture is really aware of it. The white man's gesture is welling up with incredible rapidity from his own personality, and he hasn't any control over the expression. It has an automatic, compulsive character. This is related to its extreme economy. It's so economical that it has an artistic quality. This is related to the title of the picture, because mimesis is the root of art. When this particular type of man undergoes certain kinds of stress, stimulation, or provocation, this kind of thing emerges. I don't think it's accidental; it's determined by the social totality, but it has to come out of an individual body. Unreflected social action involves a regression of the individual, an accumulating conformism. What is conformed to in this regression isn't the surface of society as much as its depths, its inner contradictions. This regression is the way individuals live the truth about society without having that truth pass through any process of reflection. Since the regression contains a truth, or involuntarily expresses one, it is a sort of inverted form of profundity. This regression can also be looked at as the subjective side of actual, objective social regression, as the consequence of the waste of human capacities which is getting worse all the time.

In both *Mimic* and *Doorpusher,* even in *Milk,* I tried to show men who retained certain capacities, skills or strengths, but who could develop no creative use for them. The "mimic" in *Mimic* is a tragic figure, in part, to me, because, as I mentioned, mimesis is the germ of art, here turned into a weapon of war. These little gestures of hate are precursors of worse things to come. The young derelict in *Doorpusher* has, as they said about safecrackers in the old movies, the "hands of a concert pianist", sensitive, capable, almost magic hands. These men have been thrown on the garbage pile, along with their natural abilities and possibilities. I don't mean to make a symmetry between victim and aggressor in the case of *Mimic,* but I want to make a very realistic image of this particular type of aggressor. By "very realistic", I mean an image which shows the inner contradictions of this figure, its socially determined quality, and also its otherness to itself.

Now, as to the question of the presence of the "opposite" to this structure of compulsion in my work: I thought for quite a while that it was first of all important to present that actuality of things, to go away from a subjectivistic dream-world of art, to show something of the dirt and ugliness of the way we have to live. So there's a negativity. I don't think I have to justify this negativity, but I will say that in my thinking about this I have been strongly influenced by the discussions and disagreements that Walter Benjamin and Theodor Adorno had during the late 1930s. Benjamin talks about the "ruins of the bourgeoisie". To me, the figure of the lower middle class and working class man, woman, or child is the most precise image of this ruin. Here we can also locate the image of the destitute person, who is always part of the working class, the sub-proletariat. But this ruined person, or ruined class, can be looked at in different, even completely opposed ways. It's very possible to use this image of a ruined class as consolation and reinforcement, to abso-

lutize the ruination of things and thereby come to the view that this is the eternal order of nature. Benjamin called this "left-wing melancholy". I feel that it is most true to see both the existing damage and at the same time to see the possibilities which have been covered over by that damage. The effects of capitalism are like scar tissue which has encrusted a living body. This living body retains the possibility to become something else, although it will have to become that carrying its scars and wounds along with it. These scars are Enlightenment. The image has to express that, too. I don't think there is a limit to the sadness we can feel when we look at the damage, but sadness, melancholy, isn't the only thing to feel in this situation.

So, in all my pictures I think there's a trace, a moment, in which there is a kind of lucid awareness of the existing unfreedom. This moment may not be identified with all the people in the picture, maybe only with some, or one. In the drama, the heavy weight of unfreedom is at the point of becoming visible, becoming an object of rational reflection. This implies that there is usually a crisis being depicted, a moment in which the personalities undergo an experience which places their existence in question. I'm trying to show this situation, this "liminal", or threshold situation, in which a person is both himself and not himself at the same instant. This non-identity with oneself is the germ of all transformation and development. It can be represented in all sorts of ways, but in photography it's especially difficult. Photography tends to show the immediate surface of the world, and so people rightly dislike it as banal, mechanical and abstract. It's not a medium in which the sense of the non-identity of a thing with itself can be easily or naturally expressed; quite the opposite. A photo always shows something resting in its own identity in a mechanical way. That's why I don't make "portraits". All the people in my pictures appear there not as themselves, but are playing the part of someone else, someone maybe not very much like themselves.

They are performing, so they are "other". I think it's possible, through the complex effects of techniques derived from painting, cinema and theatre, to infuse the photographic medium with this dialectic of identity and non-identity. And the reason I want to do this is to represent both the surface of damaged life, and its opposite, the possibility of another life, one which will come out of this one as its negation. It cannot come from anywhere else. We can imagine it, we can make pictures of it. So when we experience the picture, we experience a kind of dissociation. The key experience for modernist art is this dissociation of identity, I think. In it, we see both our actual existence for what it is and, at the same time, catch a glimpse of something extremely different. Something better.

Els Barents: When you talk about "something better" you are talking about progress, about a better world. This is an idea which is identified with an avant-garde position. This position, as you say, has been widely considered as nostalgic and invalid in today's society. But you nevertheless persist in holding on to it.

Jeff Wall: Yes, that's true. I mentioned that I thought there is a "counter-tradition" within modernity. This counter-tradition is what I identify as "avant-garde". I don't believe in the media sense of the idea of "avant-garde", the Walt Disney version. The term itself is inaccurate, with its connotations of constant, relentless, almost amnesiac forward movement. But the term has become established, and we have to use it, even though I'm not at ease with its implications.

The classically accepted concept of the avant-garde as a form of culture which centred itself in a contestation over the social value of art is one which I accept. This contestation over value is central because our society is a class-divided, antagonistic one. So there are contesting ideas in every aspect of life. There is no unity as such in capitalism, and so the representation of figures within it always contains a sense of this "otherness" we were talking about before. You can analyze the roots of this contestation, or struggle, in culture in any number of ways, but all of them, in my opinion, remain rooted in class conflict. So the analysis continuously encounters the problem of value or, if you like, the mystery of value. The mystery of value is the fundamental mythic content of modernity. Money is God, totem, fetish; what we have always thought of as mythic or totalizing thought is simultaneously an economic psychology. The grand myths of metamorphosis which lie at the basis of Western culture are, I believe, enacted anew in the production, exchange, and consumption of every commodity. The surface of life is a hieroglyphic expression of the actual value-forms in society. So representation confronts the inner nature of the social order automatically in giving its account of that surface and its relation to that surface. The question of the value of a cultural product, an image, an object, an art work, has been at the centre of the development we call the avant-garde. The ready-made,

the Productivist/Constructivist/Surrealist critique, are all incomprehensible without understanding their concentration on the problem of value. Every specific expression, every subject of a picture, to exist as a part of this tradition, is obliged to reflect on the conditions under which its social value is established. In doing so, it becomes part of the fundamental contestation over value. This gives the work of art its educative function: it creates conditions in which the inner workings of society, and therefore also the inner developments and metamorphoses of the individual psyche, can be perceived, experienced sensuously as pleasure, and at the same time can be thought of, can be reflected upon for their truth.

I don't think that an artist today can have any real motivation to investigate this problematic without having some sense of the limitations of the existing order, some sense of its disastrous character. Why try to contest, otherwise? There's plenty of decorating to be done. Having some sense of these limitations implies having the concept of an alternative. This alternative has no predetermined privileged cultural form, but it nevertheless has a role to play in culture. And that role was articulated in ways which are still important by avant-garde practice and theory.

We can't remain at the level of the historical or classical avant-garde, but at the same time we can't launch ourselves subjectively into a new epoch of some kind. I believe that the idea of a "post-avant-garde" situation is a kind of wish-fulfilment. The wish is that the kinds of contradictions and conflicts which shape culture under capitalism have been transcended, that we're in a new epoch. The new epoch has allegedly been brought about by computers, by the "failure of socialism", by all kinds of things. It's called "neo-capitalism", or "post-industrial society" or something like that. There are innumerable experts and pundits outlining this new world. People seem to be hoping that the image of capitalist modernity as the regime of unfreedom and empty suffering which was developed, in part, by the avant-garde critique has somehow been invalidated, and that therefore the whole language of this critique no longer holds good for investigating the world. I see this kind of hoping against hope as an ideological phantasm. There is still capitalism, and monopoly capitalism at that. The relations of subjection which are reproduced every time a commodity is made are still being reproduced billions of times a day. Suffering and dispossession remain at the centre of social experience. But at the same time and for the same reasons the contestation continues at every moment. This conflict is permanent in class society. It may not be so immediately visible on the surface of culture these days, but it remains in motion beneath that surface. It cannot be wished or fantasized away. It always promises to appear; avant-garde culture is based on this possibility.

The counter-tradition I'm interested in is not just an art movement, it is a whole political culture. And because its politics are based on the material possibility of change, art plays a prominent role in it. It does so because it provides this complicated glimpse of something better that I mentioned before. The glimpse of something "other" which you experience in art is always a glimpse of something better because experiencing art is, as Stendhal said, the experience of a "promesse de bonheur", a promise of happiness.

Els Barents: And how do you think your pictures, which are so attentive to the unfreedom and unhappiness of the present, give a promise of happiness?

Jeff Wall: I always try to make beautiful pictures.

LIST OF PLATES

1. The Destroyed Room 1978
   159 × 234 cm. National Gallery of Canada, Ottawa.

2. Young Workers 1978–83
   Eight portraits, each 101.6 × 101.6 cm.
   Emanuel Hoffman-Stiftung, Basel.

3. Picture for Women 1979
   163 × 229 cm.

4. Movie Audience 1979
   Seven portraits in three groups,
   each 101.6 × 101.6 cm.
   Rüdiger Schöttle, Munich.

5. Double Self-Portrait 1979
   172 × 229 cm. Art Gallery of Ontario, Toronto.

6. Stereo 1980
   Two panels. Both 213 × 213 cm.
   Left, Cibachrome transparency.
   Right, silkscreen on plexiglas.
   National Gallery of Canada, Ottawa.

7. Steves Farm, Steveston 1980
   57 × 229 cm. Edition of three.

8. The Jewish Cemetery 1980
   62 × 229 cm. Edition of three.

9. The Bridge 1980
   60 × 229 cm. Edition of three.

10. Woman and her Doctor 1980–81
    105 × 152 cm. Private Collection, Cologne.

11. Backpack 1981–82
    119 × 213 cm. Vancouver Art Gallery, Vancouver.

12. Mimic 1982
    198 × 228.6 cm. Beijer Collection, Stockholm.

13. No 1983
    228.6 × 330 cm.

14. Doorpusher 1984
    122 × 249 cm. Private Collection, Munich.

15. Bad Goods 1984
    228.6 × 347 cm. Vancouver Art Gallery, Vancouver.

16. Milk 1984
    187 × 228.6 cm. Private Collection, Cologne.

17. Diatribe 1985
    203 × 228.6 cm.

18. Abundance 1985
    122 × 222.5 cm. Private Collection, Cologne.

19. The Smoker 1986
    87.5 × 104 cm. Private Collection, Munich.

20. The Thinker 1986
    234 × 216 cm.

All works, unless specified otherwise, are Cibachrome transparencies back-illuminated with fluorescent light and mounted in display cases.

GROUP EXHIBITIONS

1969 *Focus 69,* Bau-Xi Gallery, Vancouver.
557,087, Seattle Museum of Art, Seattle.
Catalogue.
995,000, Vancouver Art Gallery, Vancouver.
Catalogue.

1970 *Four Artists: Tom Burrows, Duane Lunden, Jeff Wall, Ian Wallace,* Fine Arts Gallery
University of British Columbia, Vancouver.
Photo Show, Student Union Gallery, University of British Columbia, Vancouver.
Art in the Mind, Allen Art Museum, Oberlin College, Oberlin, Ohio. Catalogue.
Information, The Museum of Modern Art, New York. Catalogue.

1971 *Inventory,* Montreal Museum of Fine Arts, Montreal. Catalogue.
3 to Infinity, Whitechapel Gallery, London. Catalogue.
Ecological Art, Bad Salzdetfurth, West Germany.
New Art, Prague.

1973 *Pacific Vibrations,* Vancouver Art Gallery, Vancouver.

1980 *Roger Cutforth, John Hilliard, Dan Graham, Jeff Wall,* Hal Bromm Gallery, New York.
Cibachrome, National Film Board of Canada, Ottawa.
Pluralities, National Gallery of Canada, Ottawa. Catalogue.

1981 *Directions 1981,* The Hirshhorn Museum, Washington, D.C. Catalogue.
Westkunst: Contemporary Art Since 1939, Museums of the City of Cologne, Cologne. Catalogue.

1982 *Documenta 7,* Museum Fridericianum, Kassel. Catalogue.

1984 *Ein Anderes Klima / A Different Climate: Aspects of beauty in contemporary art,*
Städtische Kunsthalle, Düsseldorf. Catalogue.
Louis XIV tanzt / Louis XIV Dances, Galerie der Künstler, Munich.
Difference: On Representation and Sexuality, The New Museum, New York;
The Renaissance Society, The University of Chicago, Chicago;
The Reference Gallery, List Visual Arts Center, M.I.T., Cambridge, Mass.;

Institute of Contemporary Arts, London. Catalogue.

1985 *Rodney Graham, Ken Lum, Jeff Wall, Ian Wallace,* 49th Parallel Centre for Contemporary Canadian Art, New York.
Doppelgänger/Cover, Aorta, Amsterdam. Catalogue.
Visual Facts: Photography and Video by Eight Artists in Canada, Third Eye Centre, Glasgow; Graves Art Gallery, Sheffield; Canada House, London. Catalogue.
Nouvelle Biennale de Paris, Parc de la Villette, Paris. Catalogue.
Subjects and Subject Matter, London Regional Art Gallery, London, Ont.;
The Art Gallery at Harbourfront, Toronto;
Laurentian University Museum and Arts Centre, Sudbury;
Mendel Art Gallery, Saskatoon. Catalogue.
Aurora Borealis, Centre international d'art contemporain de Montreal. Catalogue.
The Public Art Show, Nexus Contemporary Art Centre, Atlanta, Georgia. Catalogue.

1986 *Glenn Branca/Jeff Wall,* Galerie Rüdiger Schöttle, Munich.
Making History: Recent Art of the Pacific West, Vancouver Art Gallery, Vancouver.
Prospect 86, Frankfurter Kunstverein & Schirn Kunsthalle, Frankfurt. Catalogue.
Louis XIV tanzt / Louis XIV Dances, Verein Kunsthalle Zürich, Zurich.

INDIVIDUAL EXHIBITIONS

1978 Nova Gallery, Vancouver.

1979 Art Gallery of Greater Victoria, Victoria, B.C. Catalogue.

1982 David Bellman Gallery, Toronto.

1983 The Renaissance Society at the University of Chicago, Chicago. Catalogue.

1984 *Jeff Wall: Transparencies,* Institute of Contemporary Arts, London; Kunsthalle, Basel. Catalogue.
Galerie Rüdiger Schöttle, Munich.

1985 Stedelijk Museum, Amsterdam.

1986 Galerie Johnen & Schöttle, Cologne.
Ydessa Gallery, Toronto.

PUBLICATIONS BY JEFF WALL

– *Landscape Manual,* 1969–70, Fine Arts Gallery, University of B.C., Vancouver. "To the Spectator", catalogue text, Art Gallery of Greater Victoria, Victoria, B.C., 1979.
– "Stereo", *Parachute* 22, Spring 1981, pp. 56–57. "The Site of Culture: Contradiction, Totality and the Avant-Garde", *Vanguard,* vol. 12, no. 4, May 1983, pp. 18–19.
– "Unity and Fragmentation in Manet", *Parachute* 35, Summer 1984, pp. 5–7.
– "Dan Graham's Kammerspiel", *Dan Graham,* The Art Gallery of Western Australia, Perth, 1985.
– "Dan Graham's Kammerspiel", *Real Life Magazine,* Winter 1985 (part 1) & Spring 1986 (part 2).
– "A Note on Movie Audience", *Kunstforum International* (*Res Publica* special issue), vol. 81, October–November 1985, pp. 144–145.
– "Zinnebeeldige procedures van versterving. Dan Graham's Kammerspiel" (Dutch translation) Part I, *Museumjournaal,* no. 5, 1986, pp. 216–284.

SELECTED PUBLICATIONS ON JEFF WALL

– Wheeler, Dennis: "The Limits of the Defeatured Landscape: A Review of *Four Artists*", *Artscanada,* no. 27, June 1970, pp. 51–52.
– Lippard, Lucy R.: *Six Years: The Dematerialization of the Art Object 1966–72,* Praeger, New York, 1973.
– Graham, Dan: *"The Destroyed Room* of Jeff Wall", *Real Life Magazine,* March, 1980, pp. 5–6.
– Wallace, Ian: "Revisionism and its Discontents: Westkunst", *Vanguard,* vol. 10, no. 7, September 1981, pp. 12–19.
– Kuspit, Donald B.: "Looking Up at Jeff Wall's Modern Appassionamento", *Artforum,* vol. 20, no. 7, March 1982, pp. 52–56.
– Gordon, Kim: "Unresolved Desires: Redefining Masculinity in Some Recent Art", *ZG,* no. 7, 1982.
– Wallace, Ian: "Jeff Wall", catalogue essay for the exhibition at the Renaissance Society at the University of Chicago, Chicago, 1983.
– Johnen, Jörg and Schöttle, Rüdiger: "Jeff Wall", *Kunstforum International* (*Goldener Oktober* special issue), vol. 65, September 1983, pp. 101–109.
– Kirshner, Judith: "A Blinding Light", *Real Life Magazine,* no. 11–12, Winter 1983–84, pp. 40–42.
– Wallace, Ian: "Jeff Wall's Transparencies", catalogue essay for the exhibition, *Jeff Wall: Transparencies,* Institute of Contemporary Arts, London/Kunsthalle, Basel, 1984.
– Wood, William: "Three Theses on Jeff Wall", *C* magazine, no. 3, Fall 1984, pp. 10–15.
– Barry, Judith: "Spiegelbeeld: Notities over de achtergrond van Jeff Walls dubbelzelfportret" (trans. Paul Groot), *Museumjournaal,* no. 6, 1984, pp. 354–363.
– Barents, Els: "Günther Förg en Jeff Wall: fotowerks", *Bulletin,* Stedelijk Museum, Amsterdam, September 1985.
– Newman, Michael: "Revising Modernism, Representing Postmodernism", *Postmodernism,* ICA Documents 4, Institute of Contemporary Arts, London, 1986, pp. 32–51.
– Honnef, Klaus: "Jeff Wall: Inszenierte Fotografie II", *Kunstforum International,* August–September 1986.
– Fol, Jack: "Jeff Wall: Le mur écran", *Des Arts,* no. 3–4, Autumn 1986, pp. 15–18.
– Groot, Paul: "Gebalsemd theatre. Over Jeff Wall's absurdistische fotowerken", *Museumjournaal,* no. 5, 1986, pp. 285–288.

Photo: Ian Wallace.

Front cover: *Mimic*. 1982. Detail
Back cover: *Woman and her Doctor*. 1980–81. Detail

First published in the United States of America in 1987
by Rizzoli International Publications, Inc.,
597 Fifth Avenue, New York, NY 10017

Copyright © 1986 by Jeff Wall and Schirmer/Mosel, Munich

Library of Congress Cataloging-in-Publication Data

Wall, Jeff, 1946–
Jeff Wall : transparencies.

1. Wall, Jeff, 1946– —Exhibitions.
2. Photography, Artistic—Exhibitions. I. Barents,
Els. II. Title. III. Title: Transparencies.
TR647.W34 1985   709'.2'4   86–29820
ISBN 0-8478-0792-4 (pbk.)

Printed and bound in West Germany